FEN

CARYL CHURCHILL

A Methuen New Theatrescript
published by Methuen
in association with Joint Stock Theatre Group

A METHUEN PAPERBACK

First published as a paperback original in 1983 by Methuen London Ltd, 11 New Fetter Lane, London EC4P 4EE in association with Joint Stock Theatre Group, 123 Tottenham Court Road, London W1P 9HN.

Ilona Sekacz's original music for Joint Stock's production of *Fen* is included at the end of this volume.

ISBN 0 413 52990 8

This is the script of the play as it was before the end of rehearsals for the first production. It must not be taken as the basis for future productions.

The front cover design is based on Lesley McIntyre's poster design for Joint Stock's production.

Girls' Song is based on quotations from *Fen Women* by Mary Chamberlain (Virago, 1977).

The pitchfork murder story in Scene Ten is based on material in an unpublished work by Charles Hansford.

Fen was first performed by the Joint Stock Theatre Group at the University of Essex Theatre on 20 January 1983 and opened at the Almeida Theatre, London on 16 February 1983, with the following cast:

SHIRLEY SHONA MISS CADE MARGARET	Linda Bassett
BOY ANGELA DEB MRS FINCH	Amelda Brown
JAPANESE BUSINESSMAN NELL MAY MAVIS	Cecily Hobbs
MRS HASSETT BECKY ALICE IVY	Tricia Kelly
VAL GHOST	Jennie Stoller
WILSON FRANK MR TEWSON GEOFFREY	Bernard Strother

Directed by Les Waters
Designed by Annie Smart
Lighting by Tom Donnellan
Original music by Ilona Sekacz

This play was written after a workshop in a village in the Fens.

Note on layout

A speech usually follows the one immediately before it BUT:
1 when one character starts speaking before the other has finished the point of interruption is marked / .
eg. DEB: You shut up, / none of your business.
MAY: Don't speak to your mum like that. etc
2 a character sometimes continues speaking right through another's speech.
eg. GEOFFREY: We had terrible times. If I had cracked tomatoes for my tea / I
SHIRLEY: It's easy living here like I do now.
GEOFFREY: thought I was lucky. etc

'It was work, work, work, it was all their lives.'
Retired School Teacher

'What's the point of working till you drop?'
Union Branch Secretary

'I'm the only Marxist in the Fens.'
Smallholder

'They must think I'm off the road.'
Smallholder

'If you don't believe, you don't see anything.'
Retired landworker

As the audience comes in, a BOY, *alone in a field, is scaring crows. He shouts and waves a rattle. As the day goes on his voice gets weaker till he is hoarse and shouting in a whisper. It gets dark.*

Scene One

A fen. A fog. JAPANESE BUSINESSMAN.

JAPANESE BUSINESSMAN: Most expensive earth in England. Two thousand pounds acre. Long time ago, under water like Holland. Drained by Vermuyden, clever man, Dutchman. Company of Gentleman Adventurers hired him to drain fen, 1630. Rich lords, planned to change swamp into grazing land, far thinking men, brave investors. Fishes and eels swimming here. Not true people had webbed feet but did walk on stilts. Wild people, fen tigers. King Charles wanted dry land, wanted to build capital city at Manea, sleepy village, funny idea. Fen people supported Cromwell. Didn't like drainage. Smashed dykes, broke sluices, Vermuyden's guards disappeared in mud. Wanted to keep fishes and eels to live on, no vision. King Charles lost head but now Cromwell wants to drain fens. Fen tigers angry. Refuse work on drainage. Thousand Scottish prisoners do job. Problems. Windmills. Problems. But in the end we have beautiful black earth. Very efficient, flat land, plough right up to edge, no waste. This farm, one of our twenty-five farms, very good investment. Belongs to Baxter Nolesford Ltd. which belongs to Reindorp Smith Farm Land trust, which belongs 65% to our company. We now among many illustrious landowners, Esso, Gallagher, Imperial Tobacco, Equitable Life, all love this excellent earth. How beautiful English countryside. I think it is too foggy to take pictures. Let us find teashop, warm fire, old countryman to tell us old tales.

Scene Two

WOMEN *and a* BOY *working in a row, potato picking down a field.*
VAL *thirty,* ANGELA *twenty-eight,* SHIRLEY *fifty,* NELL *forty,* WILSON *sixteen.*
MRS HASSET *forty-five, gangmaster, stands at one end of the field watching them.*
SHIRLEY *sings the fireman's song from children's TV programme Trumpton.*

SHIRLEY (*sings*):
Pugh, Pugh, Barney McGrew,
Cuthbert, Dibble, Grub.
Da da diddidi da
Diddidi diddidi diddidi da
Da da diddidi da
Diddidi diddidi da, pom.

ANGELA *joins in and sings with her.*
NELL *joins in.*
VAL *stops and stands staring.*

NELL: You all right, girl?

NELL *doesn't stop working.*
VAL *goes down the field to the end where* MRS HASSETT *is.*

MRS HASSETT: What's the matter, Val? Took short?

VAL: I've got to leave now.

MRS HASSETT: What do you mean, got to leave? It ent three o'clock.

VAL: I know, but I'm going.

MRS HASSETT: Who's going to do your work then? Mr Coleman wants this done today. How does it make me look?

VAL: Sorry, I can't help it.

MRS HASSETT: You think twice before you ask me for work again because I'll think twice an' all. So where you off to so fast?

VAL: Just back home.

MRS HASSETT: What's waiting there then?

VAL: I've got to. I've gone. Never mind.

MRS HASSETT: Wait then, I'll give you a lift halfway. I've another lot at Mason's I've got to look in on.

VAL: I've got to go now.

MRS HASSETT: You'll be quicker waiting. I don't owe you nothing for today.

VAL: You do.

MRS HASSETT: Not with you messing me about like this, not if you want another chance.

VAL: I'll start walking and you pick me up.

VAL *goes.*
The others arrive at the end of the field.
WILSON *is first.*

MRS HASSETT: What's your name? Wilson? The idea's to get the work done properly not win the Derby. Want to come again?

WILSON: Yes, Mrs Hassett.

MRS HASSETT: Because if you work regular with me it's done proper with stamps. I don't want you signing on at the same time because that makes trouble for me, never mind you. And if I catch you with them moonlighting gangs out of town you don't work for me again. Work for peanuts them buggers, spoil it for the rest of you, so keep well clear.

NELL: Spoil it for you, Mrs Hassett.

MRS HASSETT: Spoil it for all of us, Nell.

ANGELA: What's up with Val?

NELL: You've got two colour tellies to spoil.

MRS HASSETT: Think you'd get a better deal by yourself? Think you'd get a job at all?

ANGELA: Where's she gone? Ent she well?

MRS HASSETT: She don't say she's ill. She don't say what.

NELL: You paying her what she's done?

MRS HASSETT: Will you mind your own business or she won't be the only one don't get picked up tomorrow morning.

NELL: It is my business. You'd treat me the same.

ANGELA: Nell, do give over.

SHIRLEY: Come on, Nell, let's get on with it.

NELL: She treat you the same.

WILSON: If I do hers, do I get her money?

MRS HASSETT: You'll have enough to do to finish your own.

WILSON: Can I try?

MRS HASSETT: If you do it careful.

NELL: Am I crazy? Am I crazy? Am I crazy?

MRS HASSETT: I'm off now, ladies and gent. Can't stand about in this wind. I should get a move on, you've plenty to do.

ANGELA: Nell, you're just embarrassing.

MRS HASSETT *goes.* SHIRLEY *and* WILSON *have already started work.*
ANGELA *starts.*
NELL *starts.*

Scene Three

FRANK *thirty driving a tractor.*
Earphones. We can hear the music he's listening to.
The music fades down, we hear him talking to himself.

FRANK: Mr Tewson, can I have a word with you?
Yes, Frank, what can I do for you lad?
I'm finding things a bit difficult.
So am I, Frank. Hard times.
Fellow come round from the union last week.
Little fellow with a squint?
I don't hold with strikes myself.
I'm not against the union, Frank. I can see the sense of it for your big newfangle farms. Not when people are friends.
Fact is, Mr Tewson, living separate from the wife and kids I can't seem to manage.
It's lucky I'm able to let them stay on in the cottage. The council housing's not up to much eh?
I'm very grateful. But Mr Tewson I can't live on the money.
You'd get half as much again in a factory, Frank. I wouldn't blame you.
But I remember when your dad worked for my dad and you and your brother played about the yard. Your poor old brother, eh Frank? It was great we got him into that home when your mum died. We're like family. We'd both put up with a lot to go on living this good

old life here.
I hate you, you old bugger.

FRANK *hits* MR TEWSON, *that is he hits himself across the face.*

VAL *arrives with* DEB *nine and* SHONA *six. They have a suitcase. She leaves them at the side of the field with the suitcase and goes to speak to* FRANK. *She has to attract his attention, shouting. He stops the tractor, takes off the earphones.*

FRANK: What happened?

VAL: Suddenly came to me.

FRANK: What's wrong?

VAL: I'm leaving him. I'm going to London on the train, I'm taking the girls, I've left him a note and that's it. You follow us soon as you can. It's the only thing. New life.

FRANK: Where are you going to live?

VAL: We'll find somewhere together.

FRANK: How much money you got?

VAL: Fifty-six pounds. I'll get a job. I just want to be with you.

FRANK: I want to be with you, Val.

VAL: All right then.

FRANK: What am I supposed to do in London?

VAL: Where do you want to go? You say. I don't mind. You don't like it here. You're always grumbling about Mr Tewson.

FRANK: He's not a bad old boy.

VAL: He don't pay what he should.

FRANK: He was good to my brother.

VAL: I'm in a panic.

FRANK: Shall I see you tonight?

VAL: In London?

FRANK: Here.

VAL: How can I get out? I'm going crazy all this dodging about.

FRANK: Come and live with me. If you're ready to leave.

VAL: With the girls?

FRANK: With or without.

VAL: He'll never let me. He'll have them off me.

FRANK: Please do.

VAL: I suppose I go home now. Unpack.

She gets the CHILDREN *and they go.*

Scene Four

VAL *and* DEB.

VAL: You're to be a good girl and look after Shona. Mummy will come and see you all the time. You can come and see Mummy and Frank. Mummy loves you very much. Daddy loves you very much. I'll only be down the road.

DEB: I want to go on the train.

VAL: We will go on the train sometime. We can't go now. Mummy's got to go and live with Frank because I love him. You be a good girl and look after Shona. Daddy's going to look after you. And Nan's going to look after you. Daddy loves you very much. I'll come and see you all the time.

DEB: I want new colours.

VAL: You've still got your old ones, haven't you. Lucky we didn't go away, you've still got all your things.

DEB: I want new colours.

VAL: I'll get you some new colours. Mummy's sorry. Love you very much. Look after Shona.

Scene Five

VAL *and* FRANK *dance together. Old-fashioned, formal, romantic, happy.*

Scene Six

ANGELA *and* BECKY, *her stepdaughter, fifteen.*
BECKY *is standing still.* ANGELA *has a cup of very hot water.*

ANGELA: You shouldn't let me treat you like this.

BECKY: Can I sit down now?

ANGELA: No, because you asked. Drink it standing up. And you didn't call me mum.

BECKY: You're not, that's why.

ANGELA: Wouldn't want to be the mother of a filthy little cow like you. Pity you didn't die with her. Your dad wishes you'd died with her. Now drink it quick.

BECKY *takes the cup and drops it. She goes to pick it up.*

Now look. Don't you dare pick it up. That's your trick is it, so I'll let you move? I'll have to punish you for breaking a cup. That cost 67p. Why do you push me?

BECKY: Too hot.

ANGELA *fills another cup from a kettle.*

ANGELA: It's meant to be hot. What you made of, girl? Ice cream? Going to melt in a bit of hot? I'll tell your dad what a bad girl you are if he phones up tonight and then he won't love you. He'll go off in his lorry one day and not come back and he'll send for me and he won't send for you. Say sorry and you needn't drink it.

BECKY *starts to drink it.*

Faster than that. Crybaby. Hurts, does it? Say sorry now. Sorry mummy.

BECKY *stands in silence.*

I'm not bothered. No one's going to come you know. No chance of anyone dropping in. We've got all afternoon and all evening and all night. We can do what we like so long as we get your dad's tea tomorrow.

BECKY: I'm going to tell him.

ANGELA: You tell him what you like and what won't I tell him about you.

BECKY: I'll tell someone. You'll be put in prison, you'll be burnt.

ANGELA: You can't tell because I'd kill you. You know that. Do you know that?

BECKY: Yes.

ANGELA: Do you?

BECKY: Yes.

ANGELA: Now why not say sorry and we'll have a biscuit and see what's on telly. You needn't say mummy, you can say, 'Sorry, Angela, I'm bad all through.' I don't want you driving me into a mood.

BECKY: Sorry, Angela, bad all through.

ANGELA *strokes* BECKY*'s hair then yanks it.*

ANGELA: No stamina, have you? 'Sorry, Angela.' What you made of, girl?

Scene Seven

NELL *is hoeing her garden.* BECKY, DEB, SHONA *spying on her.*

DEB: Is she a man?

BECKY: No, she's a morphrodite.

DEB: What's that?

BECKY: A man and a woman both at once.

DEB: Can it have babies by itself?

BECKY: It has them with another morphrodite. Like snails. But she's never met one yet.

SHONA: Is she a witch?

BECKY: She eats little children, so watch out.

DEB: She talks to herself. That's spells.

BECKY: Angela says she makes trouble.

DEB: She goes in the gang with my mum.

BECKY: She makes trouble.

DEB: Let's get her wild.

BECKY: I hate her, don't you?

DEB: She makes me feel sick.

BECKY: Let's make her shout.

SHONA: Poo bum! Poo bum!

DEB: Shut up, Shona.

NELL: What you doing there?

BECKY: Watching you, so what?

NELL: Come out and watch me close up then.

DEB: Can I ask you something?

NELL: What?

DEB: Have you got – have you got – ?

NELL: What?

They giggle.

NELL: Well I don't know what you want. Want to help me with my garden? You can do some weeding.

BECKY: That's a funny hat.

NELL: That's a good old hat. It's a funny old hat.

SHONA: Poo bum.

NELL: You watch out, Shona, or you'll have a smack.

DEB: You hit my sister and I'll kill you.

BECKY: I'll kill you. Kill you with the hoe. You're horrible.

BECKY *takes the garden hoe and pokes it at* NELL.

NELL: Watch what you're doing. Put it down.

DEB: Make her run. Give her a poke.

BECKY: Jump. Jump.

SHONA: Poo poo poo poo.

NELL: You stop that.

NELL *grabs* SHONA, *holds her in front of her, between herself and the hoe.*

Now you mind who you poke.

SHONA *screams and struggles.*

Give me my hoe and get on home.

DEB: You let her go.

BECKY: I'll have your foot. I'll have your eyes.

NELL: Right then, you stop in there like a little rabbit.

NELL *pushes* SHONA *into a rabbit hutch.*

SHONA: Let me out.

DEB: Kill her.

BECKY: Let her out.

NELL: Give me that hoe first. Now shut up, Shona, or I'll have you for tea.

DEB: Kill her.

BECKY *screams and stabs at* NELL, *who ducks and gets her hat knocked off.*

NELL: Now give me my hoe.

BECKY *gives her the hoe.*

Give me my hat.

BECKY *gives her the hat.*

And get out of my garden.

DEB: Shona.

NELL: What if I keep Shona an hour or two? Teach you a lesson.

DEB: Please let her go.

SHONA: Deb, get me out, I can't move, get me out.

NELL: Nasty, nasty children. What will you grow up like? Nasty. You should be entirely different. Everything. Everything.

NELL *lets* SHONA *out.*

You're the poo bum now, all rabbit business.

SHONA: Are you a witch?

NELL: No, I'm a princess. Now get out.

Girl's Song (BECKY, DEB, SHONA)

I want to be a nurse when I grow up
And I want to have children and get married.
But I don't think I'll leave the village when I grow up.

I'm never going to leave the village when I grow up even when I get married.
I think I'll stay in the village and be a nurse.

I want to be a hairdresser when I grow up or perhaps a teacher.
I don't really care if I get married or be a hairdresser.

I want to be a cook when I grow up.
If I couldn't be a cook I'd be a hairdresser.
But I don't really want to leave the village when I grow up.

I don't think much about what I want to be.
I don't mind housework.
I think I want to be a housewife until I think of another job.

When I grow up I'm going to be a nurse and if not a hairdresser.

I'm going to be a hairdresser when I grow up and if not a nurse.

Scene Eight

MAY, VAL*'s mother, sixty, filling in a pools coupon.* DEB *and* SHONA *colouring.*

MAY: When the light comes down from behind the clouds it comes down like a ladder into the graveyards. And the dead people go up the light into heaven.

SHONA: Can you see them going up?

MAY: I never have. You look for them, my sugar.

A long silence.

DEB: Sing something, nan.

MAY: I can't sing, my sugar.

Silence.

SHONA: Go on, sing something.

MAY: I can't, I can't sing.

Silence.

SHONA: Mum can sing.

MAY: Yes, she's got a nice voice, Val.

DEB: Sing something.

Pause. MAY *seems about to sing.*

MAY: I can't sing, my sugar.

DEB: You're no good then, are you.

MAY: There's other things besides singing.

DEB: Like what?

Silence.
VAL *comes. They all go on with what they're doing.*

VAL: Hello, mum. Hello, Deb. Oh Deb, hello. Shona, Shona. What are you drawing? Can't I look?

MAY: They're telling me off because I can't sing. You can sing them something since you're here.

VAL: You want me to sing you something, Deb?

DEB: No.

VAL: Shona?

Pause.
VAL *starts to sing. She stops.*

MAY: How long is this nonsense going to last?

VAL: Don't.

MAY: I'm ashamed of you.

VAL: Not in front.

MAY: What you after? Happiness? Got it have you? Bluebird of happiness? Got it have you? Bluebird?

Silence.

What you after?

DEB: Shut up.

VAL: Don't speak to your nan like that.

DEB: You shut up, / none of your business.

MAY: Don't speak to your mum like that. She's getting dreadful, Val. / You've only yourself to blame.

DEB: I'm not. You are. You're getting dreadful.

MAY: You see what I mean.

VAL: You're winding her up.

MAY: I'm winding her up? She was good as gold till you come in. / You better think what you're doing.

VAL: Don't start on me. Just because you had nothing.

MAY: Don't speak to me like that, / my girl, or it's out you go.

DEB: Don't speak to my mum.

VAL: I've not been here / five minutes.

DEB: Don't speak to my nan.

VAL: Shut up, Deb.

MAY: Don't speak to the child like that.

SHONA *screams and runs off. Silence.*

Don't go after her.

VAL: Don't you go after her.

MAY: Deb, you go and look after your sister.

DEB: No.

Pause.

VAL: I'd better go after her.

DEB: Leave her alone.

MAY: Leave her alone a bit, best thing.

Silence.

VAL: Never mind, Deb.

MAY: Get one thing straight. It's no

trouble having them. They've always a place here.

VAL: I know that.

MAY: I'll stand by you. I stand by my children.

Silence.

I'd never have left you, Val.

VAL: Just don't.

MAY: I'd go through fire. What's stronger that that?

VAL: Just don't.

MAY: What's stronger?

Silence.

DEB: I'll get Shona.

Scene Nine

MR TEWSON *fifty-five and* MISS CADE, *thirty-five, from the City.*

TEWSON: Suppose I was to die. I can claim fifty percent working farmer relief on my land value.

CADE: And thirty percent on the value of your working capital.

TEWSON: My son would still have a bill of –

CADE: Three hundred thousand pounds.

TEWSON: Which I don't have.

CADE: That's the position exactly.

TEWSON: It would mean selling a hundred and fifty acres.

CADE: That's what it would mean.

TEWSON: He could do that.

CADE: It's certainly an option.

TEWSON: Take a good few generations before the whole farm disappears. Eh?

CADE: Alternatively you can give land direct to the Inland Revenue.

Pause.

Alternatively.

TEWSON: I need to be bloody immortal. Then I'd never pay tax. You're bloody immortal, eh? City institutions are immortal.

CADE: The farmers who have sold to us are happy, Mr Tewson.

TEWSON: Bloody driven to it. Don't have to like you as well. I've read about you, Miss Cade. Moguls.

CADE: The popular farming press unfortunately –

TEWSON: And tycoons. And barons.

CADE: The specialist journals take a longer view.

TEWSON: Who pushed the price of land up?

CADE: Not in fact the City.

TEWSON: I don't want these fields to be worth hundreds of thousands. More tax I have to pay.

CADE: We follow the market. The rise in prices is caused by government policies. Ever since the Heath administration introduced rollover relief –

TEWSON: Same old fields. My great great grandfather, Miss Cade.

Pause.

I am a member of the Country Landowners Association. We have ears in the corridors of power. My family are landowners. If I sell to you I become a tenant on my grandfather's land. Our president appealed to us to keep our nerve.

CADE: With us, your grandson will farm his grandfather's acres. The same number of acres. More. You'll have the capital to reinvest. Land and machinery.

Pause.

TEWSON: My family hold this land in trust for the nation.

CADE: We too have a sense of heritage.

Pause.

TEWSON: Grandson, eh?

CADE: No reason why not.

TEWSON: When I say nation. You don't want to go too far in the public responsibility direction. You raise the spectre of nationalisation.

CADE: No danger of that. Think of us as yourself.

TEWSON: No problem getting a new tractor then.

CADE: I can leave the papers with you.

TEWSON: Cup of tea? Daresay Mrs Tewson's made a cake. You want to watch the Transport and General Workers. The old agricultural union was no trouble. We'll have these buggers stopping the trains.

MISS CADE *goes.* TEWSON *is following her. He is stopped by the sight of a* WOMAN *working in the fields, a* GHOST.

TEWSON: Good afternoon. Who's that? You're not one of Mrs Hassett's girls.

GHOST: We are starving, we will not stand this no longer. Rather than starve we are torment to set you on fire. You bloody farmers could not live if it was not for the poor, tis them that keep you bloody rascals alive, but there will be a slaughter made amongst you very soon. I should very well like to hang you the same as I hanged your beasts. You bloody rogue, I will light up a little fire for you the first opportunity I can make.

TEWSON: My father saw you. I didn't believe him.

GHOST: I been working in this field a hundred and fifty years. There ain't twenty in this parish but what hates you, bullhead.

TEWSON: Are you angry because I'm selling the farm?

GHOST: What difference will it make?

TEWSON: None, none, everything will go on the same.

GHOST: That's why I'm angry, bullhead.

TEWSON: I'm going.

GHOST: Get home then. I live in your house. I watch television with you. I stand beside your chair and watch the killings. I watch the food and I watch what makes people laugh. My baby died starving.

Scene Ten

WOMEN *onion grading.* SHIRLEY, NELL, ANGELA, ALICE.

SHIRLEY: No Val today?

ANGELA: No time for onions.

NELL: Need the money though, won't she?

ALICE: Not surprised she don't come. You shouldn't be surprised.

SHIRLEY: What's that mean?

ALICE: Way you treat her.

SHIRLEY: What's that mean?

ALICE: Everyone's acting funny with her.

ANGELA: She's the one acting funny. Leave her own kiddies. If I had my own kiddies I wouldn't leave them.

ALICE: I know she's wicked but she's still my friend.

SHIRLEY: What you talking about wicked?

ALICE: It was sinners Jesus Christ come for so don't you judge.

SHIRLEY: Who said anything?

ALICE: Outside school yesterday, collecting time, no one said hello except me.

SHIRLEY: I wasn't there, was I. Expect me to shout from the other end of the street. Hello Val! Say hello now, shall I? Hello, Val! That'll cheer her up wherever she is. Altogether now, Hello –

ALICE: Never mind. You're all so – never mind.

NELL: Did I ever tell you about my grandfather?

SHIRLEY: When he was a boy and run away, that one?

NELL: I know you know, you'll have to hear it again.

ALICE: People are all miserable sinners. Miserable.

SHIRLEY: You want to tell Val not us. Give her a fright.

ANGELA: This one of your dirty stories, Nell? Or one of your frightening ones?

SHIRLEY: It's funny.

NELL: He used to swear this really happened. When he was ten his mother died in childbirth, and his father soon got a woman in he said was a housekeeper, but she slept with him from the first night. My grandfather hated her and she hated him, and she'd send him to bed without any tea, and his father always took her side. So after a few months of this, early one morning when his father had gone to work but she wasn't up yet, he took some bread and some cold tea and he run off. He walked all day and it got real dark and he was frit as hell. There was no houses on the road, just an old green drove sometimes going off towards the coast, so he thought he'd have to sleep by the road. Then he sees a little light shining so he set off down the drove that led to it and he comes to an old stone house. So he knocks on the door and the woman comes, and she'd a candlestick in one hand and a big old copper stick in the other. But when she sees it's only a boy she says come in and she makes him sit by the fire and gives him a bowl of hot milk with some fat bacon in it and a hunk of brown bread. Then she says, 'Me and my husband are going out but you can sleep by the fire. But you must stay here in the kitchen,' she says, 'whatever you do, you mustn't go through that door,' and she points to the door at the back of the kitchen. Then her husband came and said the pony trap was ready and he didn't look too pleased to see the boy but he didn't say nothing and off they went for their night out. So he sat by the fire and sat by the fire, and he thought I'll just take a look through that door. So he turned the handle but it was locked. And he saw a key lay on the dresser and he tried it and slowly opened the door, and then he wished he hadn't. There was a candle in the window which was the light he'd seen, and a long table, and on the table was a coffin with the lid off, and inside the coffin there was a body. And he was just going to shut the door and hurry back by the fire when the body in the coffin sat up and opened its eyes, and said, 'Who are you boy?' Oh he were petrified. But the body said, 'Don't be afraid, I'm not dead.' he said, 'Where have they gone?' meaning the woman and the husband. When he heard they were out he got out of the coffin and come in the kitchen and made some cocoa. Then he told my grandfather his missus had been having an affair with the chap from the next smallholding, and she was trying to get rid of him by putting rat poison in his food, and he'd fed it to some pigeons and they'd died. So what he'd done, he'd pretended to die, and she'd told the doctor he'd had a heart attack, and he'd been put in the coffin. And before that he'd sold the farm without telling the wife and had the money safe in the bank under another name. So he give my grandfather a screwdriver and said when the couple came home and screwed down the coffin, after they was in bed he was to unscrew it again. So he went back by the fire and pretended to be asleep, and he heard them screw up the coffin and laughing about how they'd got the old man's farm and kissing, and later he got the old fellow out and he were real glad because he said he wanted a pee so bad he could almost taste it. Then he got a large two tined pitchfork and a pickaxe handle and he said, 'Come on it's time to go.' My grandfather thought they were going to leave, but the old fellow crept upstairs, and gave the boy the candle and the pickaxe handle to carry, and he crept up and opened the door of the bedroom. There was the couple lying close together, completely naked and fast asleep. Then suddenly he raised the pitchfork and brung it down as hard as he could directly over their bare stomachs, so they were sort of stitched together. They screamed and screamed and he grabbed the pickaxe handle off of my grandfather and clubbed them on their heads till they lay still. Then he gets the man and takes him downstairs and puts him in the coffin and screws it up. He says, 'They'll bury him tomorrow and think it's me, and when they find her dead they'll know she was out drinking with her fellow and they'll think he killed her and done a bunk, so the police won't be looking for me,' he said, 'they'll be looking for him. And I'm going to start a new life in London or Australia, and if you talk about it I'll find you and slit your throat from ear to ear.' And he never did till he was so old he knew the old man must be dead, and even then he waited a good few years more, and I was the first person he ever told. The old fellow gave my grandfather a gold sovereign and told him to walk west and look for a job on a farm over that way, so he walked five days and slept five nights in barns, and got a job on a farm near Doncaster.

ANGELA: He never heard no more about it?

NELL: If it was in the paper he wouldn't know because he couldn't read. He never heard nothing about it, and his father never found him neither.

ALICE: You said it was funny, Shirley.

ANGELA: I don't reckon it's true.

SHIRLEY: Funny if it is true, eh Nell?

NELL: I believe it all right. Why not? There's harder things to believe than that. Makes me laugh.

Scene Eleven

SHIRLEY *working in the house. She goes from one job to another, ironing, mending, preparing dinner, minding a baby.* VAL *is there, not doing anything.* SHIRLEY *never stops throughout the scene.*

VAL: I made a cake Deb always likes and I had to throw half of it away. Frank and I don't like cake.

SHIRLEY: You're bound to miss them.

VAL: I do see them.

Silence.

It's right he should keep them. I see that. It's not his fault. He's a good father. It's better for them to stay in their own home. Frank's only got the one room. It makes sense. It's all for the best.

SHIRLEY: At harvest dad'd say, 'Come on, Shirley, you're marker.' Then if the shock fell over, 'Who's the marker?' I'd say, 'I'll go outside, let someone else be marker,' but he wouldn't let me. And leading the horse. 'What if he treads on my feet?' I never could work in front of a horse. Many's the time they'd bolt up the field. My mother wouldn't let me off. 'Just get on with it, Shirley.'

VAL: Can I help with something?

SHIRLEY: Thank you but I know how I like it.

Silence.

VAL: Is that Mary's baby?

SHIRLEY: No, it's Susan's.

VAL: You've so many grandchildren I lose track.

SHIRLEY: I'll be a great-grandmother next.

VAL: What, Sukey's never?

SHIRLEY: No, but she's sixteen now and I was a grandmother at thirty-two.

Silence.

Same thing when I went into service. I was fifteen and I hated it. They had me for a week's trial and I could have gone home at the end of it but I didn't want my mother to think she'd bred a gibber. Stayed my full year.

Silence.

I don't think she will somehow, Sukey. She's got green hair. Shocks her mother.

Silence.

Woken up, have we?

SHIRLEY *picks up the baby.*

VAL: I can't remember what they look like.

SHIRLEY: You see them every other day.

VAL: I don't think I can have looked at them when I had them. I was busy with them all the time so I didn't look. Now when I meet them I really stare. But they're not the same.

SHIRLEY: You've too much time on your hands. You start thinking. Can't think when you're working in the field can you? It's work work work, then you think, 'I wonder what the time is,' and it's dinner-time. Then you work again and you think, 'I wonder if it's time to go home,' and it is. Mind you, if I didn't need the money I wouldn't do any bugger out of a job.

VAL: Sukey's a freak round here but if she went to a city she wouldn't be, not so much. And I wouldn't.

SHIRLEY: You can take the baby off me if you want to do something.

VAL *takes the baby.*

SHIRLEY: We have to have something to talk about, Val, you mustn't mind if it's

JOINT STOCK'S NEXT TWO SHOWS

Victory, Howard Barker's latest play, opens in Brighton in February, then tours Britain and comes to the Royal Court, London in March.
Victory is a comic, bawdy, passionate play set in the chaos of the Restoration in 1660, a disorderly and scandalous epoch of English history.
Bradshaw, the widow of a Republican intellectual, discovering the fate of her husband's body, sets out on a journey of personal exploration which brings her into a number of different worlds, including the court of the new King and an English suburban garden which harbours the blind genius, Milton.

Later in 1983, Bill Gaskill will direct a new play by Nicholas Wright, based on one of Balzac's greatest novels, *Splendeurs et misères des Courtisanes*. The story of a young adventurer and two people in love with him, one a master-criminal, the other a society prostitute, the play follows the impact of his dizzying rise on the aristocrats, bankers, opportunists and outcasts who form Paris society.

JOINT STOCK THEATRE GROUP
presents
FEN
by
CARYL CHURCHILL

SHIRLEY/SHONA/MISS CADE/ MARGARET	Linda Bassett
BOY/ANGELA/DEB/MRS FINCH	Amelda Brown
JAPANESE BUSINESSMAN/NELL/ MAY/MAVIS	Cecily Hobbs
MRS HASSETT/BECKY/ALICE/IVY	Tricia Kelly
VAL/GHOST	Jennie Stoller
WILSON/FRANK/MR TEWSON/ GEOFFREY	Bernard Strother
Directed by	LES WATERS
Designed by	ANNIE SMART
Lighting by	TOM DONNELLAN
Music by	ILONA SEKACZ
Production Manager	SHEELAGH BARNARD
Stage Managers	ALAN DAY
Costume Supervisor	INGRID HASKAL
	MARION WEISE
Publicist	EDDIE TULASIEWICZ
For Joint Stock Theatre Group General Manager	LYNDA FARRAN

CARYL CHURCHILL has written two other plays for Joint Stock, *Light Shining in Buckinghamshire* (1976) and *Cloud Nine* (1979). *Cloud Nine* was first performed at the Royal Court in 1979 and revived in 1980. Since May 1981 has been playing off-Broadway in New York's Lucille Lortel Theatre. Caryl's other plays include *Owners* (Royal Court Theatre Upstairs 1972), *Objections to Sex and Violence* (Royal Court 1974), *Vinegar Tom* (Monstrous Regiment 1976), *Traps* (Royal Court Theatre Upstairs 1977), *Three More Sleepless Nights* (Soho Poly and Theatre Upstairs 1980). *Top Girls* was seen at the Royal Court in 1982, toured to Joe Papp's Public Theatre in New York with the original cast in January 1983 and returned to the Royal Court in February 1983. Her television work includes three BBC plays, *After Dinner Joke* (1978), *Legion Hall Bombing* (1978) and *Crimes* (1981).

Set built by A.M. Flint Scenery Co. with additional scenery by Ken Marples and Jason Warre. (Masks by Vin Burnham). Fight direction by Malcolm Ranson. Dialect Coaching by Joan Washington. Poster designed by Lesley McIntyre. Production photographs by John Haynes.

Joint Stock would like to thank the following for their generosity; Chingford Food Packers (onion bags): Gaskell Broadloom (carpet underlay): Islington Borough Council (hoe): The Natural Shoe Store (Shona's shoes): Nikon UK (cameras): Royal Court Theatre, London (baby): Tandy (radio-headphones): Tesco's (foodstuffs): Whitbread and Co. (beer): Zetters (pools coupons). Special thanks to Mary Chamberlain, Charles Hansford of Wisbech and to Mrs Parish of Chatteris for their invaluable help.

Joint Stock Theatre Group is subsidised by the Arts Council of Great Britain and *Fen* has received financial assistance from the Eastern Arts Association.

Joint Stock Theatre Group has been working successfully for the past nine years. Below are listed all the productions staged by the company since 1974.

	PLAY	WRITER	DIRECTOR
1974	THE SPEAKERS	Heathcote Williams	William Gaskill & Max Stafford-Clark
1975	FANSHEN	David Hare	"
1976	YESTERDAY'S NEWS	Devised by Company	"
	LIGHT SHINING IN BUCKINGHAMSHIRE	Caryl Churchill	Max Stafford-Clark
1977	DEVILS ISLAND	Tony Bicât	David Hare
	A THOUGHT IN THREE PARTS	Wallace Shawn	Max Stafford-Clark
	A MAD WORLD, MY MASTERS	Barrie Keeffe	William Gaskill & Max Stafford-Clark
	FANSHEN	Revival	
	EPSOM DOWNS	Howard Brenton	Max Stafford-Clark
1978	THE RAGGED TROUSERED PHILANTHROPISTS	Stephen Lowe	William Gaskill
1979	CLOUD NINE	Caryl Churchill	Max Stafford-Clark
1980	THE HOUSE	David Halliwell	Richard Wilson
1981	OPTIMISTIC THRUST	Devised by Company	William Gaskill
	SAY YOUR PRAYERS	Nick Darke	Richard Wilson
	BORDERLINE	Hanif Kureishi	Max Stafford-Clark
1982	REAL TIME	Devised by Company	Jack Shepherd
1983	FEN	Caryl Churchill	Les Waters
	VICTORY	Howard Barker	Danny Boyle
	LOST ILLUSIONS	Nicholas Wright	William Gaskill

you. We'll soon stop. Same things people do in cities get done here, we're terrible here, you're the latest that's all. If it's what you want, get on with it. Frank left his wife two years ago and everyone's got used to that. What I can't be doing with is all this fuss you're making.

VAL: I can't hold the baby, it makes me cry. I'll do the ironing.

SHIRLEY: Give her here then. You don't want to be so soft. If you can't stop away from them, go back to them.

VAL: I can't leave Frank.

SHIRLEY (*to the baby*): Nothing's perfect is it, my poppet? There's a good girl.

SHIRLEY*'s husband* GEOFFREY, *sixty, comes in. By the end of the scene he has had the soup she prepared.*

GEOFFREY: Dinner ready?

SHIRLEY: Just about.

VAL: Hello, Geoffrey.

GEOFFREY: Could do with some dinner.

SHIRLEY: Ent you got a civil tongue?

GEOFFREY: I don't hold you personally responsible, Val. You're a symptom of the times. Everything's changing, everything's going down. Strikes, militants, I see the Russians behind it. / All the boys want to do today

SHIRLEY: You expect too much Val. Till Susan was fifteen I never went out. Geoffrey wouldn't either, he wouldn't go to the pub without me. 'She's mine as much as yours', he say, 'I've

GEOFFREY: is drive their bikes and waste petrol. When we went to school we got beaten and when we got home we got beaten again. They don't want to work today.

SHIRLEY: as much right to stop in as what you have.

Pause.

Lived right out on the fen till ten years ago. You could stand at the door with your baby in your arms and not see a soul from one week's end to the next. / Delivery van come once a week. My sister come at Christmas.

GEOFFREY: Don't talk to me about unemployment. They've got four jobs. Doing other people out of jobs. Being a horseman was proper work, but all your Frank does is sit on a tractor. Sitting down's not work. Common market takes all the work.

Pause.

Only twenty in church on Sunday. Declining morals all round. Not like in the war. Those French sending rockets to the Argies, forgotten what we did for them I should think. / Common market's a good thing for stopping wars.

SHIRLEY: I remember dad said to mum one Bank Holiday, 'Do you want go to out?' 'Yes please,' she said. 'Right,' he said, 'We'll go and pick groundsel.'

GEOFFREY: We had terrible times. If I had cracked tomatoes for my tea / I

SHIRLEY: It's easy living here like I do now.

GEOFFREY: thought I was lucky. So why shouldn't you have terrible times? Who are all these people / who come and live

SHIRLEY: Your bike'd be mud right up to the middle of the wheel.

GEOFFREY: here to have fun? I don't know anybody. Nobody does. Makes me wild. / My mother was glad she could

SHIRLEY: I'd think, 'If anything's after me it'll have to pedal.'

GEOFFREY: keep us alive, that's all. I'm growing Chinese radishes. I've never eaten Chinese food and I never will. Friend of mine grows Japanese radishes and takes them to Bradford, tries to sell them to the Pakis. Pakis don't want them. You want to pull yourself together, girl, that's what you want to do.

Scene Twelve

WOMEN *working down the field, stone picking. Bad weather.* SHIRLEY, VAL, ANGELA, BECKY, NELL.

SHIRLEY (*sings*):
Who would true valour see
Let him come hither.
One here will constant be
Come wind come weather.
There's no discouragement
Shall make him once relent
His first avowed intent

To be a pilgrim.

It's hard singing in the wind. She's out of breath. No one joins in. A plane flies over. Only NELL *looks up.*
They go on working.
MR TEWSON *comes out to watch.*

NELL: Sod this.

ANGELA: Keep up, Beck.

They reach the end of the field one by one and stop.

TEWSON: You're good workers, I'll say that for you.

NELL: Thank you very much.

TEWSON: Better workers than men. I've seen women working in my fields with icicles on their faces. I admire that.

SHIRLEY: Better than men all right.

NELL: Bloody fools, that's all.

ANGELA: What you crying for, Beck?

BECKY: I'm not.

SHIRLEY: Cold are you?

BECKY: No.

NELL: I am and so are you. What's going to make us feel better? Sun going to come out? You going to top yourself, Tewson, like that farmer over Chatteris?

TEWSON: She's funny in the head, isn't she.

ANGELA: She likes a joke.

TEWSON: Better watch her tongue.

SHIRLEY: She's a good worker, Mr Tewson, she don't do no harm.

NELL: Don't I though. Don't I do harm. I'll do you some harm one of these days, you old bugger.

ANGELA: What you made of, Becky?

SHIRLEY: You'll get used to it.

BECKY: I want to be a hairdresser.

TEWSON: That was a friend of mine you were speaking of. He found out he had six months to live. So he sold his orchards without telling anyone. Then before he started to suffer he took his life. Never said a word to his family. Carried it out alone, very bravely. I think that's a tragedy.

SHIRLEY: Well it is, yes.

TEWSON: Might clear up tonight.

TEWSON *goes.*

NELL: Best hope if they all top themselves. Start with the queen and work down and I'll tell them when to stop.

VAL *has only now finished her piece and joins them.*

SHIRLEY: All right, Val?

NELL: What's wrong with you?

VAL: Nothing.

NELL: Slows you up a lot for nothing.

VAL: It's like thick nothing. I can't get on. Makes my arms and legs heavy.

SHIRLEY: Still you're back with the kids, best thing. Just get on with it.

VAL *starts working again.*

NELL: You think I'm the loony. Is she eating? Sleeping?

ANGELA: She wants to go to the doctor, get some valium. (*She calls after* VAL:) A man's not worth it, mate. Kids neither.

NELL: I'm not working in this.

SHIRLEY: Don't be soft.

NELL: It's more than rain, it's splinters. Come on, Becky, you've had enough.

BECKY: Can I stop, Angela? Please, mum, can I?

ANGELA: I've had enough myself. Can't work in this.

SHIRLEY: I can.

NELL, ALICE, BECKY *move off.* SHIRLEY *starts working again.* VAL *works too, slower.*

Scene Thirteen

FRANK *and* VAL.

FRANK: What?

VAL: I wanted to see you.

FRANK: Why?

Silence.

Coming back to me?

VAL: No.

FRANK: Then what? What?

Silence.

I don't want to see you, Val.

VAL: No.

FRANK: Stay with me tonight.

Silence.

VAL: No.

FRANK: Please go away.

Scene Fourteen

IVY*'s birthday.* IVY*, ninety,* MAY*'s mother.* MAY, VAL, DEB, SHONA. VAL *lights the candles on the cake, clumsily.*

IVY: Sometimes I think I was never there. You can remember a thing because someone told you. When they were dredging the mud out of the leat. I can picture the gantry clear as a bell. But whether I was there or someone told me, I don't know.

MAY: Blow your candles out, mum.

IVY: Am I ninety? Ninety is it?

They sing 'Happy Birthday'.

'Are you the bloody union man?' he'd say to Jack. 'Are you the bloody union man?' And Jack'd say, 'Are you going to pay him, because if not I'll splash it all over.'

MAY: Kiss your greatnan, Shona.

IVY: Ever kill a mouse, Shona? Tuppence a score. How old are you?

SHONA: Six.

IVY: I come home late from school on purpose so I wouldn't have to help mum with the beet. So I had to go without my tea and straight out to the field. 'You can have tea in the dark,' mum said, 'but you can't pick beet in the dark.' I were six then. Jack didn't wear shoes till he were fourteen. You could stick a pin in. Walked through the night to the union meeting. Fellow come round on his bike and made his speech in the empty street and everybody'd be in the house listening because they daren't go out because what old Tewson might say. 'Vote for the blues, boys,' he'd say and he'd give them money to drink. They'd pull off the blue ribbons behind the hedge. Still have the drink though. You'd close your eyes at night, it was time to open them in the morning. Jack'd be out in the yard at midnight. 'It's my tilley lamp and my wick,' I said, 'you owe me for that, Mr Tewson.' Chased him with a besom. 'You join that union, Jack,' I said. Nothing I couldn't do then. Now my balance takes me and I go over backwards.

DEB: Don't you like the cake?

VAL: Yes, of course.

DEB: Why don't you eat it then?

IVY: There was five of us if you count my brother John that had his face bit off by the horse. 'Are you the bloody union man?' That quack who said he could cure cancer. Took the insides of sheep and said it was the cancer he got out. I didn't believe it but most of them did. Stoned the doctor's house when he drove him out. Welcomed him back with a brass band. Laudanum pills were a great thing for pain. Walk from Littleport to Wisbech in no time.

DEB: I want to go home.

MAY: Don't be rude, Deb.

DEB: I want to go home, mum. Mum.

VAL: What?

IVY: Ninety is it? Old fellow lived next to us, he was a hundred. He'd come out on the bank and shout out to the undertaker lived on the other side, 'Jarvis, Jarvis, come and make my coffin.' 'Are you the bloody union man?' he'd say. 'Yes I am,' he'd say, 'and what about it?' They don't marry today with the same love. 'Jarvis, come and make my coffin.'

Scene Fifteen

Baptist women's meeting. MAVIS, MRS FINCH, MARGARET. VAL *and* ALICE *arrive. Happy, loving. Song: 'He's Our Lord'.*

MRS FINCH: God is doing wonderful things among us.

MAVIS: I hope you'll stay with us because we all love each other.

ALICE: She's a friend of mine. I brought her.

MAVIS: Alice is a beautiful friend to have.

They sing: 'Thank you Jesus'.
ALICE *puts her arm round* VAL.
MRS FINCH *comforts* VAL *too.*

MRS FINCH: How lovely to be here again with all my sisters. And specially lovely to welcome new faces. We hope you will commit yourself to the Lord because with him you will have everything. And without him, nothing. This is not a perfect world and we can't be perfect in it. You know how we work cleaning our houses or weeding our gardens, but they're never perfect, there's always another job to start again. But our Lord Jesus is perfect, and in him we are made perfect. That doesn't mean I'm perfect. You know I'm not. I know you're not. But we've plunged ourselves body and soul in the water of God. Next Sunday Margaret will be baptised and she'll testify before the whole congregation. Tonight she's going to share with her loving sisters how she accepted the Lord into her life.

MARGARET: I thought I would be nervous but I'm not. Because Jesus is giving me strength to speak. I don't know where to begin because I've been unhappy as long as I can remember. My mother and father were unhappy too. I think my grandparents were unhappy. My father was a violent man. You'd hear my mother, you'd say, 'Are you all right, mum?' But that's a long time ago. I wasn't very lucky in my marriage. So after that I was on my own except I had my little girl. Some of you knew her. But for those of you who didn't, she couldn't see. I thought at first that was why she couldn't learn things but it turned out to be in her head as well. But I taught her to walk, they said she wouldn't but she did. She slept in my bed, she wouldn't let me turn away from her, she'd put her hand on my face. It was after she died I started drinking, which has been my great sin and brought misery to myself and those who love me. I betrayed them again and again by saying I would give it up, but the drink would have me hiding a little away. But my loving sisters in Christ stood by me. I thought if God wants me he'll give me a sign, because I couldn't believe he really would want someone as terrible as me. I thought if I hear two words today, one beginning with M for Margaret, my name, and one with J for Jesus, close together, then I'll know how close I am to him. And that very afternoon I was at Mavis's house and her little boy was having his tea, and he said, 'More jam, mum.' So that was how close Jesus was to me, right inside my heart. That was when I decided to be baptised. But I slid back and had a drink again and next day I was in despair. I thought God can't want me, nobody can want me. And a thrush got into my kitchen. I thought if that bird can fly out, I can fly out of my pain. I stood there and watched, I didn't open another window, there was just the one window open. The poor bird beat and beat round the room, the tears were running down my face. And at last at last it found the window and went straight through into the air. I cried tears of joy because I knew Jesus would save me. / So I went to Malcolm and said baptise me now because I'm ready. I want to give myself over completely to God so there's nothing else of me left, and then the pain will be gone and I'll be saved. Without the love of my sisters I would never have got through.

VAL: I want to go.

ALICE: What? Val?

VAL: I'm going. You needn't.

ALICE: Aren't you well?

VAL: I feel sick.

ALICE: I'm coming, I'm coming.

VAL *and* ALICE *leave.*
They are outside alone. Night.

ALICE: It's a powerful effect.

VAL: Yes.

ALICE: I'm glad I brought you, Val.

VAL: I hated it.

ALICE: What do you mean?

VAL: That poor woman.

ALICE: She's all right now, thank the Lord.

VAL: She just liked a drink. No wonder.

Can't you understand her wanting a drink?

ALICE: Of course I can. So can Jesus. That's why he forgives her.

VAL: She thinks she's rubbish.

ALICE: We're all rubbish but Jesus still loves us so it's all right.

VAL: It was kind of you to bring me. I loved the singing. And everyone was so loving.

ALICE: Well then? That's it, isn't it? Better than we get every day, isn't it? How cold everyone is to each other? All the women there look after each other. I was dreadful after the miscarriage and they saved my life. Let Jesus help you, Val, because I know you're desperate. You need to plunge in. What else are you going to do? Poor Val.

ALICE *hugs* VAL.

VAL: Can't you give me a hug without Jesus?

ALICE: Of course not, we love better in Jesus.

VAL: I'd rather take valium.

Scene Sixteen

VAL *and* FRANK.

VAL: I was frightened.

FRANK: When?

VAL: When I left you.

FRANK: I was frightened when you came back.

VAL: Are you now?

FRANK: Thought of killing myself after you'd gone. Lucky I didn't.

VAL: What are you frightened of?

FRANK: Going mad. Heights. Beauty.

VAL: Lucky we live in a flat country.

Song from Rilke's Duino Elegies (ALL)

Who, if I cried, would hear me among the angelic orders? And even if one of them suddenly pressed me against his heart, I should fade in the strength of his stronger existence. For Beauty's nothing but beginning of Terror we're still just able to bear, and why we adore it so is because it serenely disdains to destroy us. Every angel is terrible. And so I repress myself, and swallow the call-note of depth-dark sobbing. Alas, who is there we can make use of? Not angels, not men; and even the noticing beasts are aware that we don't feel . . . at home in this interpreted world. There remains, perhaps, some tree on a slope, to be looked at day after day, there remains for us yesterday's walk and . . . a habit that . . .stayed . . .Oh, and there's Night, there's Night, when wind full of cosmic space feeds on our faces: for whom would she not remain, . . . painfully there for the lonely heart to achieve? Is she lighter for lovers? Alas, with each other they only conceal their lot! Don't you know *yet?* – Fling the emptiness out of your arms to broaden the spaces we breathe – maybe – the birds will feel the extended air in more fervent flight.

Scene Seventeen

VAL *and* FRANK. *Outdoors. Night.*

FRANK: What you doing?

VAL: Can't sleep.

FRANK: Come back to bed. I can't sleep with you up.

VAL: I'm not too bad in the day, am I?

FRANK: Go back to them then.

VAL: Tried that.

FRANK: He'd have you back still.

VAL: Tried it already.

FRANK: If I went away it might be easier. We'd know it was for definite.

VAL: You could always come back. I'd come after you.

FRANK: I'd better kill myself hadn't I. Be out of your way then.

VAL: Don't be stupid.

FRANK: The girls are all right, you know.

VAL: I just want them. I can't help it. I just want them.

FRANK: I left my family.

VAL: Not for me.

FRANK: I didn't say it was for you. I said I manage.

VAL: I'm the one who should kill themself. I'm the one can't get used to how things are. I can't bear it either way, without them or without you.

FRANK: Try and get them off him again.

VAL: We've been over that. They're his just as much. Why should he lose everything? He's got the place. We've been over that.

FRANK: Let's go to bed. I'm cold.

VAL: One of us better die I think.

Scene Eighteen

WOMEN *playing darts in the pub.* SHIRLEY, NELL, ALICE. ANGELA *and* FRANK *watching.*

NELL: How's Mr Tewson then?

FRANK *doesn't answer.*

You're his right-hand man.

FRANK: I do my job.

NELL: I'm nobody's right hand. And proud of it. I'm their left foot more like. Two left feet.

FRANK: Bloody trouble-maker.

NELL: I just can't think like they do. I don't know why. I was brought up here like everyone else. My family thinks like everyone else. Why can't I? I've tried to. I've given up now. I see it all as rotten. What finished me off was my case. Acton's that closed down.

FRANK: Made trouble there.

NELL: I wanted what they owed me – ten years I'd topped their effing carrots. You all thought I was off the road. You'll never think I'm normal now. Thank God, eh? Tell you something about Tewson. He's got a sticker in the back of his car, Buy British Beef. And what sort of car is it?

FRANK: Opel.

NELL: There, see?

FRANK: He's sold the farm, hasn't he? He's just a tenant himself. He had to, to get money for new equipment.

NELL: So who's boss? Who do you have a go at? Acton's was Ross, Ross is Imperial Foods, Imperial Foods is Imperial Tobacco, so where does that stop? He's your friend, I know that. Good to your brother, all that. Nice old fellow.

FRANK: That's right.

NELL: You don't think I'm crackers, do you?

FRANK: No.

NELL: I don't think you are neither. You cheer up anyway. Don't give them the satisfaction.

FRANK: I'm fine, thank you.

NELL: You never see a farmer on a bike.

NELL *goes to play darts.* ANGELA *joins* FRANK.

ANGELA: All alone?

FRANK: Just having a pint.

ANGELA: How's Val?

FRANK: Fine.

ANGELA: Never thought you were the type.

FRANK: What type?

ANGELA: After the married women.

FRANK: I'm not.

ANGELA: I got married too soon you know. I think forty-five's a good age to get married. Before that you want a bit of fun. You having fun?

FRANK: No.

ANGELA: Maybe it's gone on too long.

FRANK: Should never have started.

ANGELA: You can always try again.

FRANK: Too late for that.

ANGELA: You've got no spirit, Frank. Nobody has round here. Flat and dull like the landscape. I am too. I want to live in the country.

FRANK: What's this then?

ANGELA: I like more scenery. The Lake District's got scenery. We went there on our honeymoon. He said we were going to live in the country. I wouldn't have come. Real country is romantic. Away from it all. Makes you feel better.

FRANK: This is real country. People work in it. You want a holiday.

ANGELA: I want more than two weeks. You wouldn't consider running away with me?

FRANK: I'm thinking of killing myself.

ANGELA: God, so am I, all the time. We'll never do it. We'll be two old dears of ninety in this pub and never even kissed each other.

Scene Nineteen

ANGELA *and* BECKY. ANGELA *has an exercise book of* BECKY*'s.*

BECKY: It's private.

ANGELA: Nothing's private from me.

BECKY: Give it back.

ANGELA: Ashamed of it? I should think so. It's rubbish. And it's dirty. And it doesn't rhyme properly. Listen to this.

BECKY: No.

ANGELA: You're going to listen to this, Becky. You wrote it, you hear it. (*She reads*:)

When I'm dead and buried in the earth
Everyone will cry and be sorry then.
Nightingales will sing and wolves will howl.
I'll come back and frighten you to death.

Who? Me, I suppose. Me?

BECKY: No.

ANGELA: Who?

BECKY: Anyone.

ANGELA: Me, but you won't. You've got a horrible mind. (*She reads*:)

The saint was burnt alive
The crackling fat ran down.
Everyone ran to hear her scream
They thought it was a bad dream.

Eugh.
Oh this is very touching. (*She reads*:)

Mother where are you sweet and dear?
Your lonely child is waiting here.

BECKY: No, no, shut up.

ANGELA:
If you could see what's done to me
You'd come and get me out of here. /
My love for you is always true –

BECKY:
Mother where are you sweet and dear?
Your lonely child is waiting here.
If you could see what's done to me /
You'd come and get me out of here.
My love for you is always true
Mother mother sweet and dear.

ANGELA: You shut up, Becky. I never said you could. Becky I'm warning you. Just for that you've got to hear another one. Not a word. Now this is dirty. Wrote this in bed I expect (*She reads*:)

He pressed her with a passionate embrace
Tears ran down all over her face.
He put his hand upon her breast
Which gave her a sweet rest.
He put his hand upon her cunt
And put his cock up her.

That doesn't even rhyme, you filthy child.

He made love to her all night long.
They listened to the birdsong.

What puts filth like that into your head?
What if I showed your dad?

BECKY: No.

ANGELA: Lucky I'm your friend.

BECKY: I'll never do another one.

ANGELA: I don't care. Hope you don't. You should do one for Frank.

BECKY: I don't love Frank.

ANGELA: You love Frank, do you? I hadn't guessed that.

BECKY: I don't. I said I don't. You do.

ANGELA: What? Watch out, Becky, don't get me started. Make a poem about him dying.

BECKY: He's not dead?

ANGELA: He tried to. He took some pills, but Val got the ambulance.

BECKY: When? When?

ANGELA: I'll make one.

Frank was miserable and wished he was dead.
He had horrible thoughts in his head.
He took some pills to end his life.

Too bad he got saved by his silly wife. Not his wife.
Now he's got to go on being alive
Like all the rest of us here who survive.
I stay alive so Frank may as well.
He won't go to heaven and he's already in hell.
Poor Frank was never very cheerful –

She stops, stuck for a rhyme.

BECKY: Except when he goes to the pub and then he's beerful.

They laugh.

ANGELA:
Those pills must have made him feel sick
And wish he'd never followed his prick.

They laugh.

BECKY: That's quite good.

Silence.

ANGELA: Becky, why do you like me? I don't want you to like me.

Silence.

BECKY: Poor Frank. Imagine.

Scene Twenty

VAL *and* SHONA.

VAL: Shona. I hoped I'd see you.

SHONA: I've been to the shop for nan.

ALL: What did you get?

SHONA: Sliced loaf, pound of sausages, butterscotch Instant Whip, and a Marathon for me and Deb, I'm going to cut it in half. The warts have gone off my hands because nan said get some meat and she got some meat yesterday and it was liver and it wasn't cooked yet but she cooked it for tea but I didn't like it but I liked the bacon. She cut off a bit and rubbed it on my warts, Deb said Eugh. Then me and Deb buried it in the garden near where nan's dog's buried. There was one here and one here and another one and some more. I watched 'Top of the Pops' last night and I saw Madness. Deb likes them best but I don't.

VAL: What do you like?

SHONA: I don't like Bucks Fizz because Mandy does. She's not my friend because I took the blue felt tip for doing eskimos and Miss said use the wax ones but I have to have felt tips so I got it and Mandy says she won't choose me when it's sides.

VAL: She'll probably have forgotten by tomorrow.

SHONA: Nan says you mustn't cut your toenails on Sunday or the devil gets you.

VAL: It's just a joke.

SHONA: My toenails don't need cutting because nan cut them already. What hangs on a tree and it's brown?

VAL: What?

SHONA: Des O'Conker. What's yellow and got red spots?

VAL: The sun with measles.

SHONA: Knock knock.

VAL: Who's there?

SHONA: A man without a hat on.

VAL: What?

SHONA: Why did the mouse run up the clock?

VAL: Why?

SHONA: To see what time it is.

VAL: Shona, when you grow up I hope you're happy.

SHONA: I'm going to be an eskimo. Mandy can't because she can't make an igloo. She can come on my sledge. Nan said to be quick.

VAL: Why does an elephant paint its toenails red?

SHONA: Footprints in the butter.

VAL: No, that's how you know it's been in the fridge.

SHONA: Why then?

VAL: So it can hide in a cherry tree.

SHONA: Deb knows that one. Nan doesn't.

SHONA *goes.*

Scene Twenty-One

VAL *and* FRANK.

VAL: I've got it all worked out.

FRANK: We've both got to die is the only thing.

VAL: No, I've got to. Listen.

FRANK: No.

Pause. VAL *pulls up her shirt.*

VAL: Look. I marked the place with a biro. That's where the knife has to go in. I can't do it to myself.

FRANK: I can't even kill a dog.

VAL: I've been feeling happy all day because I decided.

FRANK: You marked the place with a biro.

VAL: I know it's funny but I want it to work.

FRANK: It's ridiculous.

VAL: Just say you love me and put the knife in and hold me till it's over.

VAL *gives* FRANK *the knife.*

FRANK: We don't have to do this.

Silence.

VAL: Say you love me.

FRANK: You know that.

VAL: But say it.

FRANK: I nearly did it. I nearly killed you.

He puts the knife down.

VAL: Do it. Do it.

FRANK: How can I?

VAL: You never do anything.

He picks up an axe.

Are you going to kill me with that?

FRANK: Will you stop talking about killing? I'm going to chop some firewood. Aren't you cold? I'm shivering. Let's have a fire and some tea. Eh, Val?

Silence.

Remember –

VAL: What?

FRANK: Early on. It wasn't going to be like this.

Silence.

Why do you – ?

VAL: What?

FRANK: All right then. All right.

He kills her with the axe.
He puts her body in the wardrobe.
He sits on the floor with his back against the wardrobe door.
She comes in from the other side.

VAL: It's dark. I can see through you. No, you're better now.

FRANK: Does it go on?

VAL: There's so much happening. There's all those people and I know about them. There's a girl who died. I saw you put me in the wardrobe, I was up by the ceiling, I watched. I could have gone but I wanted to stay with you and I found myself coming back in.

There's so many of them all at once. He drowned in the river carrying his torch and they saw the light shining up through the water.

There's the girl again, a long time ago when they believed in boggarts.

The boy died of measles in the first war.

The girl, I'll try and tell you about her and keep the others out. A lot of children died that winter and she's still white and weak though it's nearly time to wake the spring – stand at the door at dawn and when you see a green mist rise from the fields you throw out bread and salt, and that gets the boggarts to make everything grow again. She's getting whiter and sillier and she wants the spring. She says maybe the green mist will make her strong. So every day they're waiting for the green mist.

I can't keep them out. Her baby died starving. She died starving. Who?

Who?

She says if the green mist don't come tomorrow she can't wait. 'If I could see spring again I wouldn't ask to live longer than one of the cowslips at the gate.' The mother says, 'Hush, the boggarts'll hear you.'

Next day, the green mist. It's sweet, can you smell it? Her mother carries her to the door. She throws out bread and salt. The earth is awake.

Every day she's stronger, the cowslips are budding, she's running everywhere. She's so strange and beautiful they can hardly look. Is that all?

A boy talks to her at the gate. He picks a cowslip without much noticing. 'Did you pick that?'

She's a wrinkled white dead thing like the cowslip.

FRANK: What have I done, Val?

VAL: There's so many, I can't keep them out. They're not all dead. There's someone crying in her sleep. It's Becky.

FRANK: I can hear her.

VAL: She's having a nightmare. She's running downstairs away from Angela. She's out on the road but she can't run fast enough. She's running on her hands and feet to go faster, she's swimming up the road, she's trying to fly but she can't get up because Angela's after her, and she gets to school and sits down at her desk. But the teacher's Angela. She comes nearer. But she knows how to wake herself up, she's done it before, she doesn't run away, she must hurl herself at Angela – jump! jump! and she's falling – but it's wrong, instead of waking up in bed she's falling into another dream and she's here.

BECKY *is there.*

BECKY: I want to wake up.

VAL: It's my fault.

BECKY: I want to wake up. Angela beats me. She shuts me in the dark. She put a cigarette on my arm. She's here.

ANGELA *is there.*

ANGELA: Becky, do you feel it? I don't, not yet. There's a pain somewhere. I can see so far and nothing's coming. I stand in a field and think. I'm not there. I have to make something happen. I can hurt you, can't I? You feel it, don't you? Let me burn you. I have to hurt you worse. I think I can feel something. It's my own pain. I must be here if it hurts.

BECKY: You can't, I won't, I'm not playing. You're not here.

ANGELA *goes.*
NELL *crosses on stilts.*

NELL: I was walking out on the fen. The sun spoke to me. It said, 'Turn back, turn back.' I said, 'I won't turn back for you or anyone.'

NELL *goes.*
SHIRLEY *is ironing the field.*

SHIRLEY: My grandmother told me her grandmother said when times were bad they'd mutilate the cattle. Go out in the night and cut a sheep's throat or hamstring a horse or stab a cow with a fork. They didn't take the sheep, they didn't want the meat. She stabbed a lamb. She slashed a foal. 'What for?' I said. They felt quieter after that. I cried for the hurt animals. I'd forgotten that. I'd forgotten what it was like to be unhappy. I don't want to.

FRANK: I've killed the only person I love.

VAL: It's what I wanted.

FRANK: You should have wanted something else.

The BOY *who scares crows is there.*

BOY: Jarvis, Jarvis, come and make my coffin.

VAL: My mother wanted to be a singer. That's why she'd never sing.

MAY *is there. She sings.*

Girls' Song

I want to be a cook when I grow up
if I couldn't be a cook I'd be a hair – dresser
But I never want to leave the village
RECIT.
when I grow up
I don't think much about what I want to be
I dont mind housework I think I'm going to be a housewife until I think of another job.
when I grow up I'm going to be a nurse and if not a hair – dresser
I'm going to be a hair dresser
when I grow up and if not a nurse.

♩ = 112 – 126

Rilke

day There re-mains for us yesterday's walk and a habit That stayed
O and there's night
Ah
Ah
There's night
when the wind full of cosmic space
Ah
Ah
Ah
Ah
feeds on our faces
For whom would she not re-main
Ah
Ah
Ah
Ah
painfully there for the lonely heart to a-chieve
is she lighter for
Ah
Ah
Ah
Ah
lovers
Alas with each other they only con-ceal their
lot
don't you know yet
fling the emptiness
out of your arms to broaden the spaces we breathe
maybe the birds will
feel the ex-ten-ded air in more fervent flight.